JAY-Z

MEGASTAR RAPPER

Adam Sutherland

WAYLAND

D1354266

Published in 2014 by Wayland

Copyright © Wayland 2014

Wayland
338 Euston Road
London NW1 3BH

Wayland Australia
Level 17/207 Kent Street
Sydney, NSW 2000

Editor: Nicola Edwards
Designer: Paul Cherrill for Basement68

British Library cataloguing in
Publication Data
Sutherland, Adam.
 Jay Z. -- (Inspirational lives)
 1. Jay-Z, 1969- --Juvenile literature.
 2. Rap musicians-- United States--
  Biography--Juvenile literature.
I. Title II. Series
 782.4'21649'092-dc23

ISBN: 978 0 7502 8862 0

Printed in China

First published in 2012 by Wayland

Wayland is a division of
Hachette Children's Books,
an Hachette UK company.

www.hachette.co.uk

Picture acknowledgements:
The author and publisher would like
to thank the following for allowing
their pictures to be reproduced in this
publication: Cover Kevin Winter/Getty
Images; p4 Yui Mok/PA Archive/Press
Association Images; p5 Yui Mok/PA Wire;
p6 Scott Wintrow/Getty Images; p7 AP
Photo/Starpix, Kristina Bumphrey; p8
Taylor Hill/FilmMagic/Getty Images; p9
Ray Tamarra/Getty Images; p10 Al Pereira/
Michael Ochs Archives/Getty Images; p11
J. Vespa/WireImage; p12 Shareif Ziyadat/
FilmMagic/Getty Images; p13 Mark Mainz/
Getty Images; p14 Scott Harrison/Hulton
Archive/Getty Images; p15 J. Pat Carter/
AP/Press Association Images; p16 Johnny
Nunez/WireImage/Getty Images; p17
Dimitrios Kambouris/WireImage; p18
David Goldman/AP/Press Association
Images; p19 Lester Cohen/WireImage/
Getty Images; p20 WireImage/Getty
Images; p21 Kevork Djansezian/AP/Press
Association Images; p22 Andy Butterton/
PA Archive/Press Association Images;
p23 Bill Kostroun/AP/Press Association
Images; p24 Kevork Djansezian/AP/
Press Association Images; p25 AP Photo/
Ed Burke for Beyonce.com, Courtesy of
the Carter Family/AP/Press Association
Images; p26 Kevork Djansezian/AP/Press
Association Images; p27 Darryl Dyck/
The Canadian Press/Press Association
Images; p28 Themba Hadebe/AP/Press
Association Images; p29 Logan Fazio/
FilmMagic/Getty Images

Contents

Jay-Z on top

It's Saturday June 28th, 2008 at the **iconic** Glastonbury festival in Somerset, UK. The sun has set on a perfect summer day, and an estimated 180,000-strong crowd are gathered at the Pyramid stage, eagerly awaiting the festival's **headlining** act, Jay-Z.

When the multi-**platinum-selling** rapper's appearance was first announced by Glastonbury's organisers, thousands of regular festival-goers – including Oasis frontman Noel Gallagher – were outraged that a rapper should be headlining the world's favourite rock festival.

As the stage lights go down, a giant screen projects Gallagher's words: 'I'm sorry, but Jay-Z? No chance... I'm not having hip-hop at Glastonbury. It's wrong.' Then Jay-Z takes to the stage, an electric guitar hanging around his neck, and opens his show with a **tongue-in-cheek** version of one of Oasis's biggest hits 'Wonderwall'.

HONOURS BOARD
Previous Glastonbury headliners
2011 Coldplay

2010 Gorillaz

2009 Bruce Springsteen

2008 Jay-Z

2007 The Killers

Jay-Z collects an award for International Male Solo Artist at the Brit Awards in 2010. The suit and tie became a trademark outfit from the release of his debut album, Reasonable Doubt.

Instantly winning over the crowd, Jay-Z switches to his own song '99 Problems' and performs a near faultless set that has become a piece of pop culture history. 'The show was one of the highlights of my career,' Jay-Z remembered later. 'It was one of those moments that taught me there really is no limit to what hip-hop could do, no place that was closed to its power.'

If any rapper could take on the rock establishment and win, it's Jay-Z – rap icon, businessman, trailblazer, trendsetter and million dollar brand. Jay-Z was the kid from the wrong side of the tracks, who grew up without a father and dropped out of school to sell drugs, before discovering a way out of the **ghetto** through an overwhelming talent for music.

He is now the man who has sold 50 million albums worldwide, who has won 15 **Grammy Awards,** who put a $5m (£3.2m) wedding ring on Beyoncé's finger, and who even owns his own basketball team!

Here we look at Jay-Z's life, his musical adventures, and his multi-million dollar business deals – from trainers to T-shirts, hotels to bars and restaurants. Want to know about the real Jay-Z? Read on...

Jay-Z's Glastonbury performance in 2008 brought acceptance of hip-hop to a traditionally rock audience.

WOW!

Jay-Z's Glastonbury performance has received over one million hits on YouTube.

Growing up in the projects

Jay-Z was born Shawn Corey Carter on December 4th, 1969 in the crowded Marcy Houses council estate known as 'the projects' in Bedford-Stuyvesant, a borough of New York City. The youngest of four children, he has two sisters, Michelle and Andrea, and a brother, Eric. A bright, lively boy, Jay-Z taught himself to ride a bike at four years old, and by six was matching pupils twice his age in school IQ tests.

TOP TIP

As a teenager Jay-Z used to read a dictionary in bed to learn new words he could put in his rhymes.

New York in the 1970s was the birthplace of hip-hop music. As young as nine, Jay-Z remembers watching older boys standing in groups 'battling' each other over the quality of their rhymes. The young man was quickly hooked, and started to carry a pen and notebook wherever he went to scribble down new ideas and phrases.

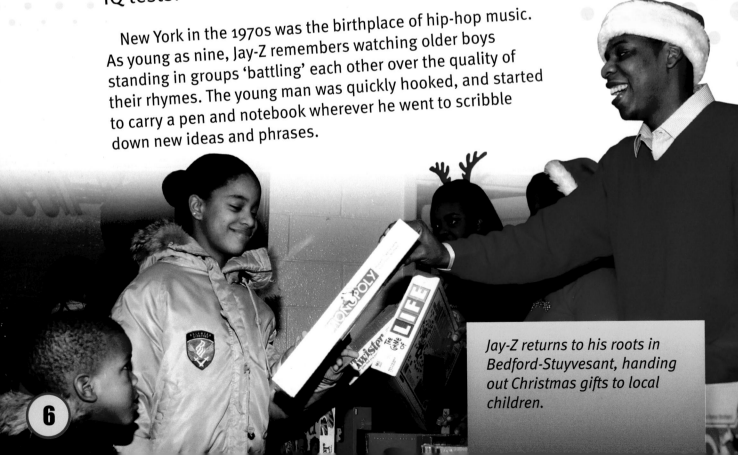

Jay-Z returns to his roots in Bedford-Stuyvesant, handing out Christmas gifts to local children.

In 1980, Jay-Z's uncle was murdered, and his father Adnis Reeves left the family to try and find the killer. Consumed with a desire for revenge, Adnis sadly descended into alcohol and drug addiction and never returned to the family home. Alone, with four young mouths to feed, Jay-Z's mother Gloria struggled to put food on the table, and Jay-Z often spent evenings at his friends' houses, just to get something to eat.

Jay-Z was devastated at the loss of his father – his school grades dropped dramatically, and he became distant from his mother. 'I changed a lot,' Jay-Z recalls. 'I became more guarded. I never wanted to be attached to something and get that taken away again.'

Searching for a male role model, he met Jonathan 'Jaz-O' Burks, a local rapper four years older than himself. Jaz-O spotted the younger boy's natural talent and took him under his wing, helping him refine his lyrics, and teaching him the basics of performing in front of an audience. Jaz-O is also able to explain his **protégé's** nickname, claiming it comes from a shortening of the childhood nickname Jazzy. Jay-Z was on his way.

Jay-Z and his mother Gloria Carter host a fundraising event for the Shawn Carter Foundation, which provides college scholarships to poor students.

HONOURS BOARD
The early hip-hop records that inspired Jay-Z
Funky Four Plus One More 'That's The Joint'
Run DMC 'It's Like That'
Afrika Bambaataa 'Looking for the Perfect Beat'
Herbie Hancock 'Rockit'
Melle Mel 'The Message'

The wrong side of the law

In the 1980s, America was overrun with a cheap and highly addictive new drug called crack cocaine. It seemed like everyone Jay-Z knew was either selling it or taking it. The young man faced a tough choice.

Jay-Z's school years were spent at George Westinghouse High School in Brooklyn. Westinghouse had one of the most dangerous reputations in the whole of America. Muggings and violence against pupils and staff were an everyday occurrence.

By the time he was 18, Jay-Z had dropped out of high school. He moved out of New York to live with an old friend from Marcy Houses, DeHaven Irby, who had relocated to Trenton, New Jersey, an hour south of the city.

HONOURS BOARD

Jay-Z's early guest appearances

Jaz-O 'The Originators'
Big Daddy Kane 'Show and Prove'
Big L 'Da Graveyard'
Mic Geronimo 'Time to Build'

A talented basketball player, DeHaven had moved schools to take advantage of a superior high school training programme in the nearby state. But in reality, he found the attraction of making money from selling drugs too hard to resist. DeHaven quickly introduced his friend to the 'hustler' lifestyle that still features in many of Jay-Z's songs.

Jay-Z is joined onstage by a group of students from Westinghouse High School in Brooklyn, the rapper's former high school.

Luckily for the young rapper, music proved to be a way out. In 1988 his former **mentor** Jaz-O signed a record deal with a UK record label, who flew him to London for two months to record an album. Jaz took the 19-year-old Jay-Z to England with him to record guest raps on the CD, and experience the lifestyle of a best-selling rapper!

Back in the US, established rap artist Big Daddy Kane heard a mixtape that Jay-Z had recorded, and asked the young man to join his US tour. For four months in 1989, Jay-Z travelled around the US as part of Kane's show, performing for little more than a bed for the night and three meals a day. The young man – who could earn several thousand dollars per week hustling on street corners – had never been happier!

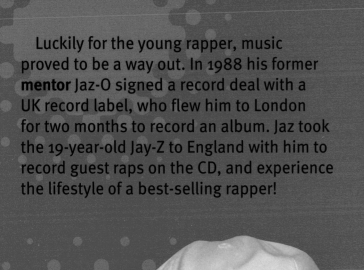

INSPIRATION

'Big Daddy Kane had an incredible amount of showmanship – even today I use some of the ideas I picked up back then about pacing and performance in my own live show.' **Jay-Z**

Rapper Jaz-O was an invaluable help to the young Jay-Z's career.

A brush with death

Jay-Z had one foot in hip-hop, but one foot still in the street. The music business was where his heart lay, but could he make a living at it?

At the end of the Big Daddy Kane tour, Jay-Z found himself back in Trenton, working the same New Jersey street corners with DeHaven. From time to time he went into the recording studio with old friends like Jaz-O to record guest verses, but he never seriously believed that music was a way out of his current lifestyle.

In 1992, DJ Clark Kent was hired by Atlantic Records, and put in charge of signing new talent. Kent had first heard Jay-Z rapping in the Marcy Houses when he was just 15, and had never forgotten the young man's jaw-dropping lyrical twists and turns. Kent tracked him down and, against the rapper's protests, eventually persuaded Jay-Z to spend more time in the recording studio, and less time hustling.

Early days: Jay-Z proudly displays his gold chain and gold tooth alongside fellow rappers Jaz-O and Queen Latifah (centre).

WOW!

Jay's first official rap single was called 'I Can't Get With That', released in 1994.

Though he was interested in music, Jay-Z saw it as a bigger gamble than his street life, which was making him a guaranteed income. However, two incidents made up his mind to pursue music full time. In 1994, Jay-Z was shot at during a street argument. Several shots were fired at close range before the gun jammed, allowing the rapper to literally escape with his life.

Secondly, around the same time, Kent introduced Jay-Z to a young Harlem **entrepreneur** called Damon Dash. At the time, Dash was a local club promoter with a talent for **marketing**. Kent believed that with a top-class talent like Jay-Z to promote, he would let the world know about the rapper's gifts. The pair bonded immediately, and Damon Dash became a major influence on Jay-Z's musical career and business life for several years to come.

Jay-Z and his former business partner Damon Dash. Dash taught Jay the basics of business, and the rapper was quick to put them into practice.

INSPIRATION

When he met Jay-Z, Damon Dash managed a group called Future Sound, and made a living as a club promoter. He generated great word-of-mouth publicity for his events by giving away extravagant gifts – like bottles of expensive champagne – to the first 100 people to arrive. Everyone wanted to attend a Dash event!

Making history

With Damon Dash on his team, and money earned on the street to spend on recording sessions, Jay-Z started work on an album that would become a hip-hop classic.

Even 20 years ago, recording an album cost a lot of money – studios charged $2,500 (£1,600) per hour for a minimum of four hours, permission to use samples (the snippets of old songs that you often hear on rap records) might cost $5,000-15,000 (£3,100-9,500) per track, and top producers often asked for $5,000 (£3,200) per song, plus a share of CD sales.

Jay-Z dug deep into his pockets, and by the end of 1995 had recorded the majority of his debut album, *Reasonable Doubt*. The album mixed great radio-friendly production with Jay-Z's unique tales from the street – the struggle to get out of the projects and be able to afford the finer things in life that the rapper has returned to throughout his career.

INSPIRATION

Resonable Doubt's 'D'Evils' is about two friends who fall out over power and money. 'When people say hustling is easy money,' says Jay, 'they couldn't be more wrong. Paranoia and fear worm their way into every interaction you have. It can wear you down.'

Magic touch: Jay-Z celebrates the tenth anniversary of Reasonable Doubt's release at a special event in New York City.

Jay and Dash played the album to all the major record labels but the realistic content of the lyrics scared a lot of record executives, and they couldn't get a deal – not even at Atlantic Records, where Clark Kent had found and **nurtured** Jay's talent.

Undeterred, the pair teamed up with a third friend Kareem 'Biggs' Burke and formed their own label Roc-A-Fella Records (a play on John D Rockefeller, the world's first billionaire). They printed copies of the album, along with T-shirts, flyers and so on – all with their own money – and started selling to fans out of the back of their cars.

Eventually, with the **hype** growing, Roc-A-Fella signed manufacturing and distribution deals with other labels, meaning stores across the US could finally stock the CD. Most importantly, though, Roc-A-Fella retained control of the **master recordings** and demanded a 50% split of profits (rather than the standard royalty rate of 20%). It was a groundbreaking deal, and a sign of Jay-Z's intelligent business dealings to come.

Jay-Z takes to the stage in New York's Times Square in 2002 to promote Roc-A-Fella's latest release.

WOW!

On *Reasonable Doubt*, Jay-Z recorded a song called 'Twenty-Two Twos' in which he repeats the words 'two', 'to' and 'too' 22 times in one verse.

Hitting the big time

With fans and critics alike praising *Reasonable Doubt* as a standout hip-hop release, it was time for Jay-Z and Damon Dash to reach for bigger and better things.

Jay-Z collected together some major talent for his debut – from producer DJ Premier to rapper Notorious B.I.G. and singer Mary J Blige. The album reached number 23 on the US Billboard 200 chart, and was later named in *Rolling Stone* magazine's '500 Greatest Albums Of All Time'.

Out of a desperate desire to get signed, most artists give away a huge percentage of the rights to their recordings. Just as they had held their nerve in controlling their own masters, however, Jay and Dash also showed the **foresight** to only agree a one-album distribution deal for *Reasonable Doubt*. They were now free to search for a new and better deal backed by the success of Jay's **debut**.

Jay-Z performs tracks from his US Billboard number 1 album Vol 2... Hard Knock Life *in 1999.*

INSPIRATION

'Jay learned a lot from [Damon]. If you're [friends] with somebody who's doing smart things, you become smarter instantly, because you watch the smart things... If you see it, you understand it.' **Russell Simmons, co-founder of Def Jam**

The pair eventually struck a deal with rap label Def Jam, which again broke the record industry mould. Rather than 'sign' Jay-Z and pay him a royalty fee based on estimated sales of future releases, Def Jam bought a 33% stake in Roc-A-Fella for $1.5m (£950,000) and **acquired** a portion of the rights to Jay-Z's future recordings but did not own them. Def Jam would also cover all production costs for Jay's albums and videos. And because Def Jam only owned one third of Roc-A-Fella, they also received just one-third of the profits, leaving Jay-Z and Dash with a massive 67% – three times more than the standard record deal!

Sitting pretty on what was undoubtedly one of the best recording contracts ever negotiated, Jay-Z went straight back into the studio and started work on his follow-up album, *In My Lifetime Vol 1*, which was released in 1997. Produced by Sean 'P Diddy' Combs, the album consciously softened Jay's sound to reach a larger audience.

The following year Jay released his third album *Vol 2... Hard Knock Life*, which became his most successful release to date. Including a track 'Hard Knock Life' that sampled a track from the Broadway musical *Annie*, it was a great mixture of crowd-pleasing melodies and harder rhymes that *In My Lifetime* had lacked. Jay-Z was now an established recording artist.

Jay-Z holds an armful of MTV Video Music awards in 2004. He won them all for his '99 Problems' video.

WOW!
Vol 2...
Hard Knock Life sold five million copies in the US. Thanks to his large percentage of royalties, it earned Jay-Z a massive $20m (£12.6m)!

Developing new artists

With Jay-Z's own recording career going from strength to strength, he and Damon Dash took the opportunity to build Roc-A-Fella as a home for other talented artists.

No one in the music business would have been surprised if Jay and Dash had used Roc-A-Fella purely as a money-making machine to line their own pockets. But the two men were dedicated to discovering, developing and promoting the best new talent they could find.

Early additions to the Roc family were rappers Beanie Sigel (who appeared on Jay's *Vol 2...*) and Memphis Bleek (who made a guest appearance on *Reasonable Doubt*). Jay-Z made a point of including his label mates on his own tours to increase their fan base, and also appeared on at least one track of each of his artists' albums. This support helped push Sigel's debut album sales over a million copies.

Jay first introduced rapper Memphis Bleek on the album Reasonable Doubt. *Here the pair perform together ten years later, in 2006.*

TOP TIP

Roc-A-Fella bought a white Mercedes E-class with a Roc logo on the bonnet to send to record stores and radio stations to promote their releases. It made Roc-A-Fella stand out from the crowd!

Jay-Z and fellow rapper (and former producer) Kanye West share a joke. Jay-Z's Roc-A-Fella label gave West his own solo deal.

Around this time, Damon Dash became interested in film production and persuaded Jay-Z to star in a straight-to-DVD release in 1998 called *Streets Is Watching*. Jay-Z also recorded the film's soundtrack. The film was certainly no Oscar winner, but it made Roc-A-Fella $2m (£1.25m) and inspired Dash to release a documentary of Jay's Hard Knock Life tour called *Backstage*.

Probably the biggest act discovered by Roc-A-Fella was producer and rapper Kanye West. West's involvement with the label dates back to 2000, when he was one of a number of guest producers on Jay-Z's *The Dynasty: Roc La Familia* CD. West then took on main production duties for Jay-Z's next album *The Blueprint* in 2001, before eventually released his own debut album *College Dropout* in 2004.

Though Jay initially needed convincing that the super-talented producer could cut it as a rapper, it was Roc-A-Fella that gave West his solo record deal, and the two men still record and perform together often, most recently on 2011's **collaboration** *Watch The Throne*.

HONOURS BOARD
Best-selling
Roc-A-Fella albums
Kanye West *College Dropout*
Beanie Sigel *The Truth*
Cam'ron *Come Home With Me*
Foxy Brown *Broken Silence*
The Diplomats *Diplomatic Immunity*

A day in the life of Jay-Z

As a rapper and businessman, two days in Jay-Z's life are rarely the same. But as President of Def Jam he experienced the 9-to-5 working life of a record executive – with a difference.

For three years, from 2005-2007, Jay-Z was the head of Def Jam Records (see pages 26-27). The rapper **commuted** to work from his apartment in **Tribeca** to the Def Jam office on 8th Avenue, just a 10-minute drive north into New York's Garment District.

According to an interview with *The New York Times*, Jay-Z woke up early, and started the day with breakfast at 8am followed by a workout in the gym. Because a lot of his Def Jam staff worked late nights, scouting new bands, Jay-Z didn't arrive at his office until 11am. Dress could be anything from a sharp suit to shorts and a polo shirt. But whatever he wore, Jay-Z was all about business.

Competition between record companies is fierce, and if Jay-Z was introduced to a new artist he liked, he kept them in his office until they had signed a contract. Rapper Tru Life remembers arriving at 3pm, and leaving 10 hours later, with the ink drying on a fresh contract. Jay-Z always got his man!

WOW!

Jay-Z's most successful signing at Def Jam was Rihanna. The Barbadian singer has sold over 25 million album sales, and 60 million singles!

Talking business: Jay-Z shares breakfast with the mayor of New York, Michael Bloomberg (centre) and Brooklyn Nets' co-owner Mikhail Prokhorov (far left).

Jay-Z's day was usually one meeting after another. He might catch up with his **A&R** team to discuss a possible new signing to the label, or meet with a Def Jam artist to choose the next single from their album, or decide which producer to use on a specific track.

Lunch was usually taken at the rapper's own 40/40 Club in Chelsea, just a few blocks from the office. After lunch, it was more deals and decisions – planning Def Jam promotional tours across the US, TV filming schedules for the label's artists, or approving cover art for DVD releases.

So many meetings can get monotonous, so when he first arrived at the record label, Jay-Z made strenuous efforts to keep his team fresh and enthusiastic. He organised team-building exercises, and even a week-long 'retreat' where execs competed to win $5,000 (£3,200) to win a record deal for a fictional singer. Jay-Z was no ordinary chief executive!

From street corner to centre stage: Jay-Z joins actor Justin Timberlake and US talk show host Jimmy Fallon at an awards show.

INSPIRATION

In 2010, Jay-Z was named in the top 10 Company Directors in the US along with Ralph Lauren, Michael Dell of Dell Computers, and Howard Schultz of Starbucks.

Jay and Dash soon realised that wearing a particular brand of clothing for a music video, or name-dropping a pair of trainers in a song, gave huge publicity for that brand. So they decided to cash in!

At the end of the 1990s, Jay and Dash became big fans of the Italian fashion label Iceberg. Iceberg was a knitwear company that had recently expanded into jeans and sportswear, and Jay-Z and other Roc-A-Fella artists were often seen wearing their clothes at concerts and events, and even dropped Iceberg's name into a few songs.

Dash was convinced that Roc-A-Fella's unofficial **endorsement** had helped boost Iceberg's sales, but when he sat down with Iceberg's management team, he discovered that rather than enter into business with the rapper, they were nervous of attaching themselves to black urban culture, and actually wanted to distance themselves from the hip-hop lifestyle.

Walking billboard: Jay-Z shows off a Rocawear T-shirt at a store opening in New York City.

TOP TIP

'We shouldn't let other people make money off us, and we shouldn't give free advertising with our lifestyle.'
Damon Dash

It was then that Jay-Z and Dash decided to start their own clothing brand, Rocawear. They bought three sewing machines for the Roc-A-Fella office, and started releasing T-shirts with a crude Roc-A-Fella logo stitched on the front. 'We didn't know how to sew,' laughs Jay, 'and we didn't really know people who knew how to sew!'

The pair quickly took advice from fellow hip-hop **mogul** and founder of Phat Farm clothing, Russell Simmons. Simmons put them in touch with business partners who had experience of the clothing business, and rather than carry on producing clothes themselves, Jay and Dash sold **licences** to established clothing companies to produce clothes featuring the Rocawear logo. Jeans and sweatshirts were the first items available, followed by footwear and children's clothes. Within 18 months of launch, Rocawear had sold $80m (£52m) worth of clothes!

WOW!

In 2005 Jay-Z and his partners paid $22m (£14m) for Damon Dash's share of Rocawear. A year later they sold the brand for $204m (£128.5m)!

Rocawear on the catwalk: the brand started making T-shirts to promote music releases and grew to be worth hundreds of millions of dollars.

Selling the lifestyle

With the success of Rocawear, Jay-Z and Dash realised that **cross-promoting** other brands in songs and videos could help launch several other businesses.

Jay-Z wasn't the first rapper to praise the quality of a certain pair of trainers in a song, wear a favourite brand at a concert, or even drive a particular make of car in a video. However, he was one of the first rappers to really treat this brand 'endorsement' as a business. He and partner Damon Dash came to the conclusion, 'We're helping the brand, so the brand should help us!'

The rapper is also a master of timing, and often combined the marketing of new music with the release of new product lines. In April 2003, Jay-Z teamed up with Reebok to release the S. Carter training shoe – complete with a CD of sneak-peek samples of his forthcoming album, *The Black Album*. The first 10,000 pairs of $150 (£95) shoes sold out in an hour. It was Reebok's fastest-selling trainer ever!

Jay-Z shows off the new Reebok S. Carter training shoe – a range he co-designed with the sportswear label.

WOW!

Jay-Z's marketing team once designed a colour called 'Jay-Z blue' to be used on cars!

As a **diehard** sports fan, Jay-Z often raps about his support for baseball team, the New York Yankees. In 2010 he partnered with the Yankees to launch a line of branded merchandise, including an official 'S. Carter' Yankees top. The obsession with sport didn't stop there, however. In 2004, basketball-mad Jay-Z was one of the investors in a successful bid to buy the New Jersey Nets – and became one of the few musicians to own a stake in a professional sports team, now called the Brooklyn Nets.

Over time, Jay-Z has widened his range of investments to include the 40/40 chain of sports bars, US cosmetics brand Carol's Daughter, and even a Michelin-starred restaurant The Spotted Pig in New York. The success of these brands became less about the promotion that Jay-Z could give them in his music, and more about how their association with the famous and successful entrepreneur and rap icon would boost brand awareness and sales. As Jay-Z put it himself, 'I'm not a businessman. I'm a business, man.'

HONOURS BOARD
Jay-Z's list of brand investments
40/40 sports bars
9IX aftershave
Carol's Daughter cosmetics
Brooklyn Nets basketball team
J Hotels
Armadale Vodka

Jay-Z and wife Beyoncé sit courtside at a New Jersey Nets versus New York Knicks basketball game. The rapper is a co-owner of the Nets.

Crazy in love

In 2002, Jay-Z asked Destiny's Child lead singer Beyoncé Knowles to appear on a new song he was recording. The collaboration eventually led to wedding bells.

Jay-Z asked Beyoncé to sing on the track '03 Bonnie & Clyde' because, in his own words, he was looking for 'an exceptional performer'. He also wanted someone with a **mainstream** Top 40 audience to help his own music cross over into the pop charts. The 'Bonnie & Clyde' video showed the pair as fictional boyfriend and girlfriend – a fiction that soon became fact!

By the summer of that year newspapers around the world were reporting that Jay-Z and Beyoncé were a couple. Like David and Victoria Beckham before them, a relationship between these two famous people wasn't twice as interesting to the press – it was ten times as interesting! By 2006 the pair were listed as the world's most powerful couple for *TIME* magazine's 100 most influential people of the year, but nevertheless worked very hard to keep much of their private life out of the papers.

HONOURS BOARD

'They're the president and first lady of the music industry.'
Jim Jonsin, record producer

Jay-Z and Beyoncé perform their hit single, 'Crazy In Love' at the BET Awards in Los Angeles in 2003.

Even their marriage in 2008 was kept such a closely guarded secret, that few people knew it had happened until after the event. The ceremony, which took place in Jay-Z's apartment in New York, was a private affair, only attended by close friends and family. In fact, Beyoncé didn't show off her wedding ring in public until September!

Though they have recorded together only rarely, their relationship has undoubtedly widened the audience for their music – Jay-Z fans can happily check out Beyoncé's latest release, and vice versa. By January 2009, Forbes ranked the pair as Hollywood's top-earning couple, with a combined total of $162m (£102m).

The latest chapter in Jay-Z and Beyoncé's love story is the birth, in January 2012, of the couple's first child, daughter Blue Ivy Carter. Who would bet against another singer in the family?

WOW!

For a wedding present, Beyoncé bought Jay-Z a $2m (£1.3m) sports car, the Bugatti Veyron Grand Sport.

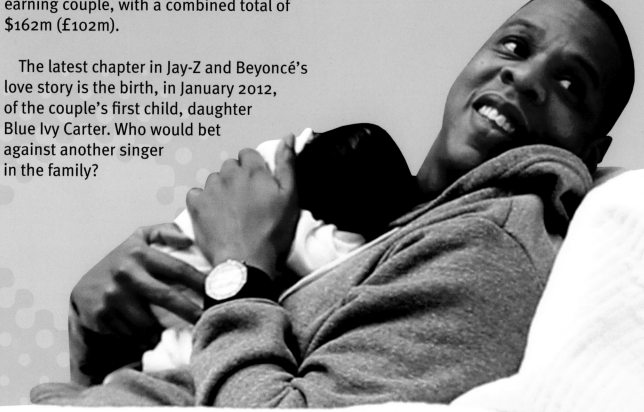

Holding the baby: Jay-Z pictured with his daughter Blue Ivy Carter, born in January 2012.

Changing the game again

In 2005, Jay-Z took a break from recording to run the Def Jam record label. Then he returned with a bang – and one of the biggest recording contracts in history.

In less than a decade as a recording artist, Jay-Z had released ten albums and sold over 33 million copies. After *The Black Album* hit the streets, Jay announced he was going to retire from hip-hop, and intended to spend more time on his business interests.

Not surprisingly, record labels were keen to **harness** his experience and 'magic touch' when it came to discovering and developing new talent. Def Jam, the label that was home to Roc-A-Fella Records pounced, offering Jay a three-year contract as the label's president on a reported salary of $8m-$10m (£5m-6.3m) per year. Just as **lucrative**, Def Jam would return the rights to all the rapper's master recordings after ten years.

Once in the hot seat at Def Jam, Jay-Z got to work revitalising the once-great record label – motivating staff, bringing in fresh ideas, and most importantly scouting new talent. One of his greatest discoveries was Rihanna, who auditioned in his office as a nervous 17 year old in 2005. Jay was so impressed, he wouldn't let the singer leave until three in the morning when a contract had been drawn up and signed!

Jay-Z and Rihanna, who he signed to the Def Jam record label, collect a Grammy Award for Rihanna's song 'Umbrella' in 2008.

By 2006, Jay-Z was getting the itch to record and perform again. In November that year he released the album *Kingdom Come*, which sold over two million copies, and in January 2007 he decided not to renew his contract with Def Jam, and returned to hip-hop full time.

In April 2008, Jay once again made music business history by announcing a groundbreaking deal with concert promoter LiveNation worth $150m (£95m) over ten years. This new deal brought Jay's recorded music, touring and record label under one roof and paved the way for other artists to sign what became known as '360 degree' deals. Jay-Z was back where he belonged – in the spotlight!

HONOURS BOARD

Facts and figures behind the LiveNation deal

- $10m upfront fee for new album, *The Blueprint 3*
- $30m upfront fees for three further CDs over ten years
- $25m 'signing' fee
- $20m for a share of the publishing and licensing rights to Jay-Z's songs
- $50m start-up fee for a new record label and talent agency, Roc Nation
- $25m upfront fees for the costs of touring/performing
- 775,000 shares in LiveNation (worth an estimated $12m)

WOW!

Jay-Z's average earnings per live show total over $1m (£630,000).

Jay-Z rocks a festival crowd in 2008. The rapper is one of the most successful live artists in the world.

The impact of Jay-Z

Jay-Z has enjoyed an extremely successful career, but has never forgotten where he came from. He makes great efforts to share that success with people less fortunate than himself.

In 2003, Jay-Z and his mother Gloria Carter launched the Shawn Carter Foundation (www.shawncartersf.com) to provide college scholarships to needy students across the US. In their first year, they provided 50 scholarships to students – one in each state of America! Since then, the Foundation has helped over 750 students, and gifted over $1.3m (£825,000).

In 2005 Jay-Z and close friend Sean 'Diddy' Combs pledged $1m (£635,000) to the American Red Cross' **relief fund** in the wake of Hurricane Katrina. The following year, the rapper visited Africa as a guest of the United Nations, and was made aware of the acute water shortages in parts of the continent. He made a documentary for MTV, *Diary Of Jay-Z: Water For Life*, and on his return met UN Secretary General Kofi Annan and pledged his support to the United Nations' mission to raise awareness.

INSPIRATION

'Empire *State* of Mind' was the last Number One hit of the 2000s. It was written by two homesick Brooklyn residents. Jay–Z rewrote all the verses but kept the chorus. The song won two Grammy Awards!

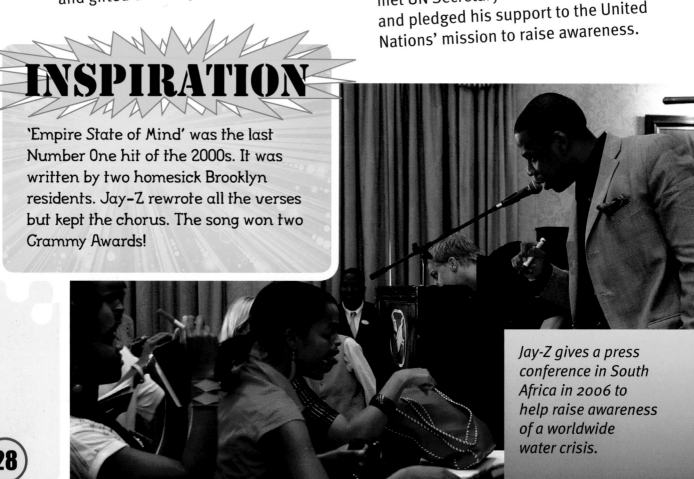

Jay-Z gives a press conference in South Africa in 2006 to help raise awareness of a worldwide water crisis.

Though admitting to never voting until he was well into his twenties, Jay-Z got actively involved with politics during the 2008 US presidential election campaign. He enthusiastically supported Democratic candidate Barack Obama and spent time working with the HeadCount organisation, which encourages young people to register to vote. He was invited to the **White House** after Obama was elected, and describes the President as a hip-hop fan. 'When I called him he was playing *The Blueprint* in the gym!'

Despite his other commitments, Jay-Z has also found the time to continue innovating and entertaining musically. His 2009 album *The Blueprint 3* was one of his most successful both commercially and critically, and 'Empire State Of Mind', the song he created for his home city, will be remembered for as long as Frank Sinatra's classic 'New York, New York'. In 2011 he released *Watch The Throne*, a new chart-topping album collaboration with fellow Roc-A-Fella artist Kanye West, and shows no sign of slowing down. Long live Jay-Z!

WOW!

'Rosa Parks sat so Martin Luther King could walk. Martin Luther King walked so Obama could run. Obama's running so we all can fly.'

Jay-Z on the 2008 US Presidential election

Jay-Z and friend Sean 'Diddy' Combs address supporters at a rally for Barack Obama's 2008 presidential campaign.

Have you got what it takes to be a million dollar brand?

1) Are you interested in music?
a) I LOVE One Direction! But apart from that, not really.
b) I like to keep up to date with the Top 40 releases, but to be honest I spend more time on Skype or XBox.
c) Absolutely! I know all the latest releases, and keep on top of industry gossip by reading loads of music blogs.

2) Have you ever tried rapping?
a) Noooo, I'd be far too embarrassed!
b) I tried it once at karaoke, but I couldn't get the words out fast enough.
c) Yes! I write my own rhymes, and I spend a lot of time repeating them until the flow is right. I'm ready to battle!

3) Do you like performing in front of an audience?
a) Argh! I hate being on stage – it's my worst nightmare.
b) I'm usually in the school play – as the back end of a donkey!
c) Love it! I'm quite a shy person, but when I'm on stage I come to life. I must be a big show off at heart.

4) Do you enjoy dreaming up new ways to make money?
a) Nah, I get £5 a week pocket money and that's all I need.
b) I once washed the neighbours' cars to get some spending money for a family holiday, but that's as far as it went.
c) All the time! I try and think about what people need – sweets, CDs, new trainers – and work out how I can supply them and make some money for myself.

5) Do you like taking risks?
a) I like playing truth or dare. Does that count?
b) I once bet my friend he wouldn't walk home from school with his shirt on back to front. I lost!
c) Of course, doesn't everyone? The greater the risk, the greater the potential reward!

6) Are you prepared to work hard in order to be successful?
a) How hard? I'm not sure I have much time to spare between finishing my homework and *The Simpsons* starting.
b) I don't mind hard work – one or two nights a week. But I tend to have other commitments too, like football practice.
c) Yes! Give me a task to do, and I'll stick with it until it's finished – no matter how long it takes. I know hard work is the key to success.

RESULTS

Mostly As: Sorry to say this, but it doesn't look like you're ready to follow in Jay-Z's footsteps just yet. You have other priorities, and don't have a strong enough interest in music – listening to it, or making it – to succeed in a very tough market.

Mostly Bs: You're interested in music, and you have the makings of an entrepreneur, but you probably need to work on your focus and drive to really succeed in the music business.

Mostly Cs: It sounds like you have what it takes to be a million dollar brand! Keep working on your music, and pushing yourself hard to succeed, and who knows?

Glossary

A&R Short for 'artist and repertoire', the people at record companies who find and sign new artists.

acquired Bought or obtained something.

collaboration The job of working with someone else to produce something, such as a new song.

commuted Travelled between home and work.

cross-promoting Using one product (e.g. a song or music video) to promote or advertise another, different product (e.g. shoes or clothes).

debut First public performance.

diehard Describes someone who continues to strongly support something despite problems or disappointment.

endorsement A declaration of someone's public support or approval for something.

entrepreneur A person who sets up a business in the hope of making a profit.

foresight The ability to predict what will happen in the future.

ghetto A part of a city occupied by a minority group, especially a slum area.

Grammy Award A musical achievement award granted by the American National Academy of Recording Arts and Sciences.

harness To make use of something, profit from it.

headlining act The band or artist who is the star attraction at an event.

hype Intensive publicity or promotion.

iconic Describes something that is memorable, deserving of high status.

licence Permission to create an official product using a brand name or logo.

lucrative Profitable, worth a lot of money.

mainstream Ideas or tastes that are shared by the majority of people.

marketing The business of promoting and selling products or services.

master recording The original recording from which all copies are made.

mentor Someone who supports and encourages someone younger or less experienced than themselves.

mogul An important or powerful person.

nurture To care for and encourage the growth or development of something.

platinum-selling To be classified as a 'platinum' release, a CD needs to sell over 1 million copies.

protégé Someone who is supported or guided by an older, more experienced person.

relief fund A system of financial help (usually set up for an urgent crisis or on-going difficulty).

tongue-in-cheek Describes something done for ironic or insincere reasons.

Tribeca An area in Manhattan, the name of which comes from 'triangle below Canal Street'.

White House The official home of the President of the United States, in Washington, DC. USA.

Index